Animal Structures

Claws, Nails, and Hooves

Heather Funk Gotlib

Cavendish Square

New York

Published in 2019 by Cavendish Square Publishing, LLC
243 5th Avenue, Suite 136, New York, NY 10016
Copyright © 2019 by Cavendish Square Publishing, LLC

First Edition

Library of Congress Cataloging-in-Publication Data

Names: Gotlib, Heather Funk, author.
Title: Claws, nails, and hooves / Heather Funk Gotlib.
Description: First edition. | New York : Cavendish Square, 2019. | Series: Animal structures | Includes index.
Identifiers: LCCN 2018023590 (print) | LCCN 2018025747 (ebook) | ISBN 9781502641755 (ebook) |
ISBN 9781502641748 (library bound) | ISBN 9781502641724 (pbk.) | ISBN 9781502641731 (6 pack)
Subjects: LCSH: Hoofs--Juvenile literature. | Claws--Juvenile literature. | Nails (Anatomy)--Juvenile literature. |
Animals--Adaptation--Juvenile literature. | Adaptation (Biology)--Juvenile literature.
Classification: LCC QL942 (ebook) | LCC QL942 .G68 2019 (print) | DDC 591.47/9--dc23
LC record available at https://lccn.loc.gov/2018023590

Editorial Director: David McNamara
Copy Editor: Nathan Heidelberger
Associate Art Director: Alan Sliwinski
Designer: Megan Metté
Production Coordinator: Karol Szymczuk
Photo Research: J8 Media

Printed in the United States of America

Contents

Animals can have **claws**, **nails**, or **hooves**.

Claws, nails, and hooves help animals use their hands and feet.

Some animals have claws.

Cats have claws.

Claws are very sharp.

Claws help them hunt.

Claws cut into things.

They let animals dig and climb.

People have nails.

Monkeys have nails.

11

Nails keep hands safe.

They can be a **tool**.

13

Some animals have hooves.

Hooves help them walk.

Horses have hooves.

15

Hooves are very hard.

They protect feet.

17

Claws, hooves, and nails have many uses.

They help animals move, hunt, and dig.

Claws, hooves, and nails help keep animals safe.

They help them survive!

21

New Words

claws (KLAHWS) The sharp parts of an animal's fingers and toes.

hooves (HUHVS) The thick bottom parts of an animal's feet.

nails (NAYLS) The hard tips of an animal's fingers and toes.

tool (TOOHL) An object you can use to help you do something.

Index

23

About the Author

Heather Funk Gotlib lives in Kentucky with her husband and daughter. She works in a museum teaching kids when she is not writing. She loves animals and has a dog and a cat.

About BOOKWORMS

Bookworms help independent readers gain reading confidence through high-frequency words, simple sentences, and strong picture/text support. Each book explores a concept that helps children relate what they read to the world they live in.